You're in for a ReTreat!

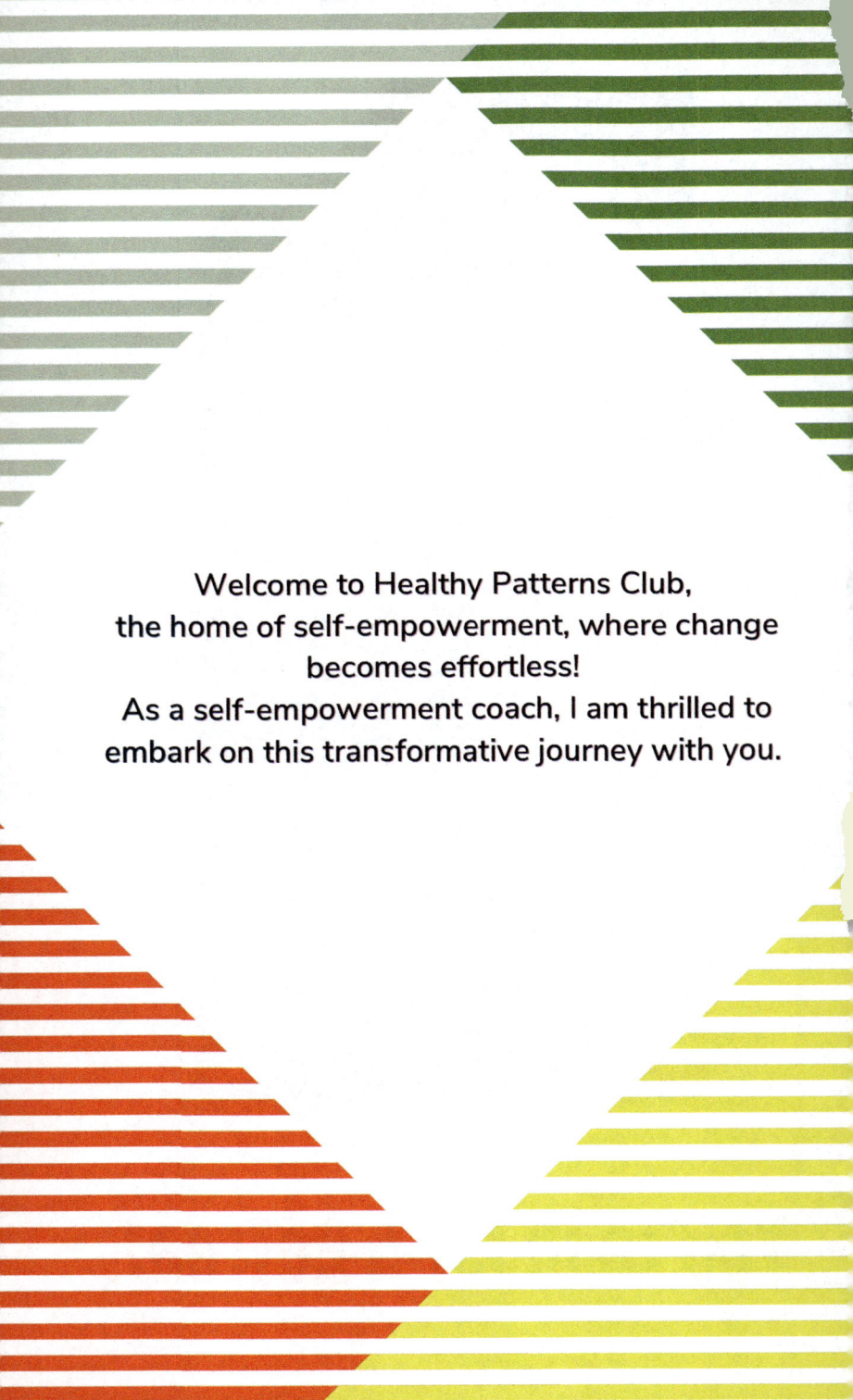

Welcome to Healthy Patterns Club,
the home of self-empowerment, where change
becomes effortless!
As a self-empowerment coach, I am thrilled to
embark on this transformative journey with you.

Healthy Patterns Club was born from my quest for inner peace, balance, and happiness. Together, we will unleash your true potential and create a life that reflects your authentic self. Leave behind the chains of the past and step into a future filled with limitless possibilities.

This 30-day mind, heart, body and soul decluttering challenge is your independent voyage of self-discovery, guided by my expertise and energetic support. With each step you take, you'll witness profound shifts in your self-image, self-worth, and overall well-being.

Throughout our collaboration, we will challenge limiting beliefs, explore new perspectives, and unlock the door to your hidden strengths and talents. As your coach, I am here to provide you with the tools, insights, and encouragement needed to navigate this journey of self-empowerment.

Remember, this is your unique adventure tailored to embrace your inner strength. Take only what resonates with you, welcome the exercises that ignite your soul, and let go of anything that no longer serves you. It's time to travel light, release the weight of self-doubt, and embrace your authentic power.

Prepare to bid farewell to your comfort zone as we embark on this exciting transformational journey together. You have all the resources within you to create a life that radiates self-confidence, self-love, and self-worth. Let's kick some buts and rewrite the script of your life with audacity and courage.

Throughout this 30-day challenge, I will be your steadfast ally, supporting you every step of the way. I have been on this path before and know now it is more than possible. Trust in yourself and the process. Embrace the magic that unfolds as you tap into your true potential and witness the extraordinary gift of growth that awaits you.

Get ready to embrace the exhilarating path of self-empowerment. As your coach, I am honoured to guide you, inspire you, and celebrate your triumphs along the way. You will create a powerful and authentic existence that reflects the radiant being you indeed are.

Table of Contents

08 - WEEK 01

SELF-AWARENESS & REFLECTION

38 - WEEK 02

CHALLENGING NEGATIVE BELIEFS

74 - WEEK 03

CULTIVATING SELF-COMPASSION & GRATITUDE

103 - WEEK 04

EMPOWERING ACTIONS & ENVIRONMENT

125 - WEEK 05

INTEGRATION & CELEBRATION

Are you ready to embark on this life-changing journey of self-empowerment?

Your transformation starts now.
Let's dive in and start creating the life you desire.

Week 1

Self-Awareness and Reflection

Reflection is the practice of introspection and contemplation. It involves deeply examining and exploring your thoughts, emotions, and experiences. Reflection creates a space for self-inquiry and self-understanding, allowing you to clarify your beliefs and their origins.

Through daily reflection, you'll engage in activities such as journaling, contemplative exercises, or self-assessment. This process encourages you to examine your self-image and self-worth from various angles, exploring the roots of negative beliefs and their impact on your life. Reflection provides an opportunity to challenge those beliefs, question their validity, and seek alternative perspectives that promote self-empowerment and self-acceptance.

Self-awareness and reflection work hand in hand. By cultivating awareness, you can observe and recognize negative thoughts and beliefs as they arise. This heightened awareness becomes the foundation for meaningful reflection, enabling you to explore the origins and effects of those thoughts and beliefs more profoundly.

Through self-awareness and reflection, you gain valuable insights into the intricate layers of your self-image and self-worth. This self-awareness helps you identify patterns, triggers, and self-sabotaging behaviours, leading to a greater understanding of yourself and the factors that have influenced your self-perception.

I encourage you to embrace the practices of self-awareness and reflection throughout this challenge. Cultivate the habit of observing your thoughts, emotions, and beliefs with curiosity and non-judgment. Set aside dedicated time for reflection, allowing yourself to dive into the depths of your self-image and self-worth.

Remember, self-awareness and reflection are ongoing processes. Each day brings new opportunities for self-discovery and growth. You will lay a strong foundation for the transformation ahead by consistently engaging in these practices. Let's explore the depths of your self-perception and unlock your limitless potential.

As your coach throughout this 30-day challenge, I'm here to "energetically" support you on your journey of self-discovery and growth. So let's dive deeper into the concepts of self-awareness and reflection and how they contribute to this transformative process.

Self-Awareness is the foundation upon which personal growth is built. It involves consciously observing your thoughts, emotions, and behaviour patterns without judgment or attachment. Developing awareness allows you to gain insights into the underlying beliefs and thought patterns that shape your self-image and self-worth.

During this challenge, self-awareness serves as your compass, guiding you to identify negative or limiting beliefs about yourself. By becoming aware of these thoughts, you can shine a light on their existence and impact on your life. Awareness helps you recognize the patterns and triggers perpetuating negative self-perception, enabling you to interrupt and change them.

Preparation

The integrated journal provides a safe space to express your thoughts, emotions, and insights, allowing you to gain more profound clarity and understanding.

Setting aside a designated time for daily tasks and exercises creates a sacred space for personal growth and self-discovery. You can choose a time of the day that works best for you, whether in the morning, during a quiet moment in the afternoon, or before bed. I firmly believe consistency is essential, so could you set up a routine supporting your commitment to this journey?

By dedicating yourself to regular journaling and committing to a specific task time, you create a supportive structure that nurtures your growth and ensures you make the most out of this challenge. Your journal will become a treasured companion, capturing your insights, breakthroughs, and moments of empowerment along the way.

DAYS 1-3 Mindful Observation

Practice mindfulness and observe your self-image and self-talk.

Day 1: Mindful Observation of Body Appreciation

Prompt: Engage in mindful observation of your body and appreciate its unique qualities and capabilities.

Journaling Tips:

Find a quiet and comfortable space to relax and focus your attention inward.

Begin by taking a few deep breaths to centre yourself and bring awareness to the present moment.

Gently bring your attention to your body. Notice its sensations, how it feels in this moment, and any areas of tension or relaxation.

Observe different body parts, starting from your head and moving down to your toes. Notice any physical sensations or feelings that arise.

Write about your observations, focusing on aspects of your body that you appreciate and the sensations that bring you a sense of gratitude or contentment.

I'd like you to reflect on how mindful observation enhances your self-image and self-worth and contributes to a greater connection with your body.

Day 2: Mindful Observation of Self-Care Practices

Prompt: Be mindful of your self-care practices and their impact on your body's self-image and self-worth.

Journaling Tips:

Set aside time for self-care activities that nurture your body and well-being.

Choose a self-care practice, such as taking a warm bath, practising yoga, or enjoying a nourishing meal.

Before engaging in the practice, take a moment to observe your intentions and expectations.

Engage in the self-care practice mindfully, paying attention to each sensation, movement, or taste involved.

Afterwards, reflect on how the practice made you feel. Notice changes in your body, mood, or overall sense of self-worth.

Write about the impact of this self-care practice on your body's self-image and self-worth, acknowledging the importance of prioritizing self-care in nurturing a positive relationship with your body.

Day 3: Mindful Observation of Inner Qualities

Prompt: Be mindful of your inner qualities and strengths contributing to your self-worth beyond physical appearance.

Journaling Tips:

Create a peaceful environment for self-reflection.

You can begin by focusing on your breath, allowing it to anchor you in the present moment.

Shift your attention to your inner qualities and strengths. Notice the characteristics that make you unique, such as kindness, resilience, creativity, or compassion.

Please observe how these inner qualities manifest in your daily life and interactions with yourself or others.

Write about the moments when these inner qualities have positively impacted your self-worth and how they contribute to a healthier and more balanced self-image.

Reflect on how cultivating awareness of your inner qualities can deepen your self-appreciation and reinforce a positive relationship with your body.

DAYS 4-6 Journaling

Reflect on your self-image and self-worth.

Write down any recurring negative thoughts or beliefs you identify.
Explore their origins and the impact they have on your life.

Day 4: Exploring Body Appreciation

Prompt: Reflect on the positive aspects of your body that you appreciate. Focus on what your body enables you to do, how it supports you, and the unique qualities it possesses.

Journaling Tips:

Start by taking a few deep breaths to centre yourself and create a calm mind.

Could you list at least three physical attributes or features of your body that you appreciate?

For each attribute or feature, explore why it is valuable and how it contributes to your overall well-being and self-worth.

Reflect on moments when your body has shown resilience, strength, or beauty. Write about those experiences and the emotions they evoke.

Please go ahead and finish your journaling session by expressing gratitude for your body and the incredible ways it supports you.

Day 5: Challenging Body Image Beliefs

Prompt: Identify any negative or limiting beliefs you hold about your body image. Take this opportunity to challenge and reframe those beliefs to promote a healthier and more positive self-image.

Journaling Tips:

You can begin by creating a safe and non-judgmental space for self-reflection.

Write down any negative beliefs you have about your body image. Be honest and specific.

Please review each belief and ask yourself if it is based on accurate information or if societal standards, comparison, or personal insecurities influence it.

Challenge each belief by providing evidence or alternative perspectives that counteract the negativity. Reframe the thoughts into positive and empowering statements about your body image.

Conclude by writing down the new, positive beliefs you want to embrace and affirm moving forward.

Day 6: Cultivating Self-Worth Beyond Appearance

Prompt: Explore the aspects of yourself that contribute to your self-worth beyond physical appearance. Focus on your inner qualities, strengths, and achievements that make you unique and valuable.

Journaling Tips:

Begin by grounding yourself and creating a sense of self-acceptance and self-compassion.

Could you make a list of five qualities or strengths that you have beyond physical appearance? These could be personal qualities, talents, skills, or achievements.

Reflect on how each quality or strength enhances your self-worth and contributes to your identity and fulfilment.

Write about moments when these inner qualities and strengths have positively influenced your life or the lives of others.

Could you conclude by confirming your worthiness beyond physical appearance and acknowledging the richness of your character and the value you bring to the world?

Remember, journaling is a personal and introspective practice. Feel free to adjust the prompts and tips to suit your preferences and needs. The key is to approach journaling with an open mind, compassion for yourself, and a willingness to explore and nurture your body's self-image and self-worth.

Journal

Week 2

Challenging Negative Beliefs

Negative beliefs are deeply ingrained thoughts or perceptions about ourselves, often based on distorted or inaccurate information. They can stem from various sources, such as childhood experiences, societal conditioning, past failures, or critical feedback from others. These beliefs can manifest as self-doubt, low self-esteem, or feelings of unworthiness, and they often act as barriers to our personal growth and professional success.

Challenging negative beliefs involves actively questioning their validity and replacing them with more empowering and realistic thoughts. Here's why this process is so important:

Self-Limiting Nature: Negative beliefs limit our potential and hinder our progress. They create a self-imposed barrier that prevents us from fully embracing our strengths, pursuing our goals, and taking risks. By challenging these beliefs, we open ourselves up to new possibilities and allow ourselves to grow beyond our perceived limitations.

Distorted Perceptions: Negative beliefs often distort our perception of reality. They can magnify our flaws, dismiss our accomplishments, and undermine our self-worth. Challenging these beliefs helps us gain a more balanced and accurate perspective of ourselves, enabling us to recognize our strengths, acknowledge our achievements, and embrace our inherent worthiness.

Self-Fulfilling Prophecy: Negative beliefs have a way of becoming self-fulfilling prophecies. When we hold onto these beliefs, we subconsciously act in ways that align with them, reinforcing the negative cycle. By challenging and changing these beliefs, we can break free from self-sabotaging patterns and create a positive upward spiral that aligns with our true potential.

Emotional Well-being: Negative beliefs contribute to feelings of self-doubt, anxiety, and low self-esteem. They can significantly impact our emotional well-being and overall quality of life. Challenging these beliefs promotes emotional healing, resilience, and a greater sense of self-compassion and self-acceptance.

Empowering Mindset: By challenging negative beliefs, we cultivate an empowering mindset that supports our personal growth and success. We learn to question the validity of our negative self-perceptions, replace them with positive and realistic thoughts, and develop a stronger belief in our abilities and worthiness.

To challenge negative beliefs effectively, it is essential to question their origins, examine the evidence supporting or refuting them, and consciously choose alternative, empowering beliefs. This process involves self-reflection, seeking evidence from past successes and positive feedback, and engaging in positive affirmations and self-talk.

I encourage you to approach the process of challenging negative beliefs with curiosity, self-compassion, and patience. Remember that changing long-held beliefs takes time and effort, but with consistent practice and dedication, you can transform your self-perception and create a more empowering and positive mindset.

DAYS 7-9 Thought Restructuring

Identify and challenge negative beliefs about your self-image and self-worth each day.

Write down evidence against the belief and develop positive, realistic counter-thoughts.

Day 7: Identifying Negative Thoughts & Beliefs

Could you take a moment to consider your thoughts about your body and identify any negative or critical ones?

Journaling Tips:

Find a quiet and comfortable space to reflect without distractions.

Take a few deep breaths to centre yourself and bring awareness to the present moment.

Observe your thoughts about your body without judgment. Write down any negative or critical reviews that come to mind.

I'd like you to reflect on how these thoughts contribute to a negative self-image and impact your self-worth.

Please look at the origins of these thoughts, such as societal influences or personal experiences, and note them in your journal.

Day 8: Challenging Negative Thoughts & Beliefs

Prompt: Challenge the negative thoughts about your body and reframe them into more positive and empowering perspectives.

Journaling Tips:

Create a calm and accepting space for your journaling practice.

Please look at the negative thoughts you identified on Day 7 and choose one to focus on.

Examine the evidence supporting and contradicting this negative thought. Write down alternative perspectives that counteract its negativity.

Reframe the negative thought into a positive and empowering statement about your body's self-image and self-worth.

I'd like you to reflect on how embracing these new perspectives can help improve your overall self-image and enhance your self-worth.

Here are a couple of examples of how to reframe negative thoughts and beliefs.

Negative thought: "I dislike my body because it doesn't look like the ideal beauty standards."

Reframed thought: "My body is unique and beautiful in its own way. It deserves love and appreciation for all that it does for me. I embrace my body's individuality and celebrate its strength and resilience."

Negative thought: "I feel ashamed of my body because it doesn't match societal expectations."

Reframed thought: "I reject societal expectations and choose to honour and accept my body as it is. I am more than my appearance, and I recognize my worth lies in my qualities, achievements, and how I treat myself and others."

Negative thought: "I compare myself to others and feel inadequate because my body doesn't measure up."

Reframed thought: "I release the need to compare myself to others. Each body is unique, and I am on my journey of self-love and self-acceptance. I celebrate my progress and nurture a positive relationship with my body."

Remember, these reframed thoughts are meant to inspire and empower you. Feel free to personalize them to align with your own experiences and values. The goal is to challenge negative thoughts and replace them with affirming and empowering beliefs that support a healthier body self-image and enhance your self-worth.

Day 9: Cultivating Positive Affirmations

Prompt: Create positive affirmations that reinforce a healthy and positive body self-image and enhance your self-worth.

Journaling Tips:

Find a peaceful environment where you can reflect and engage in positive affirmations.

Please look at the reframed thoughts from the previous day and identify the most empowering ones.

I'd like you to write these positive affirmations, focusing on your body's self-image and self-worth.

Repeat these affirmations to yourself, both in your mind and aloud, with conviction and belief.

Please reflect on the impact of these positive affirmations on your self-perception and self-worth, and note any shifts or changes you experience.

Remember, thought restructuring takes time and practice. Be patient and gentle with yourself as you challenge negative thoughts and cultivate positive perspectives. We will go deeper into structuring and mastering powerful positive affirmations in the coming days!

Example:

Original Thought: "I'm not good enough. I always fall short of expectations."

Restructured Thought: "I am enough just as I am. I acknowledge my unique strengths and accomplishments and am constantly growing and evolving."

DAYS 10-12   Affirmation Practice

Create positive affirmations related to self-image and self-worth.
Repeat them daily to reprogram your thoughts.

Day 10: Identifying Affirmation Areas

Prompt: Reflect on body self-image and self-worth areas you want to affirm and enhance.

Affirmation Areas:

Physical Appearance: Affirmations about embracing and appreciating your body's physical attributes.

Inner Qualities: Affirmations about acknowledging and celebrating your inner qualities, strengths, and resilience.

Self-Care and Nurturing: Affirmations focused on practising self-care, self-compassion, and nurturing your body and mind.

Journaling Tips:

Create a calm and inviting space where you can reflect and journal.

You can begin by exploring each affirmation area and writing down specific qualities or aspects you want to affirm.

I'd like you to reflect on why these qualities or aspects are essential to you and how affirming them can enhance your body's self-image and self-worth.

Could you write a list of positive affirmations for each affirmation area based on the qualities or aspects you identified?

You can choose one or two affirmations from each area that resonate most with you for further practice.

Day 11: Embracing Affirmations

Prompt: Practice embracing and internalizing the positive affirmations you have identified.

Journaling Tips:

Find a peaceful and comfortable space where you can focus on your affirmations.

Take a few deep breaths to centre yourself and create a calm mind.

Please repeat your chosen affirmations silently or aloud, focusing on each individually.

Reflect on the meaning and truth behind each affirmation. Visualize yourself embodying those qualities and experiences.

I'd like you to please write about any emotions, sensations, or shifts in mindset that arise as you engage with the affirmations.

Day 12: Integrating Affirmations into Daily Life

Prompt: Explore ways to integrate your positive affirmations into your daily life for lasting impact.

Journaling Tips:

I'd like you to reflect on how you can incorporate affirmations into your daily routine and mindset.

Could you write down specific actions or practices you can engage in to reinforce and embody your affirmations?

Could you create affirmation cards or reminders that you can place in visible locations as visual cues throughout the day?

Reflect on challenges or resistance when integrating affirmations and identify strategies to overcome them.

I'd like you to write a personal commitment statement expressing your dedication to practising and embodying these affirmations daily.

Remember, cultivating positive affirmations takes time and consistency. Be patient and kind to yourself throughout this process. Adjust the prompts and tips to suit your needs and preferences. The key is to approach affirmations with a mindful and open mindset, embracing their power to enhance your body's self-image and self-worth.

Here are a few examples of positive affirmations to support you on your journey.

"I am worthy of love, respect, and happiness exactly as I am.

"I embrace my unique qualities and celebrate the person I am becoming."

"I acknowledge my worthiness and value and deserve all life's good things."

Journal

Power tips on how to structure powerful positive affirmations.

Structuring positive affirmations is a simple and effective way to create powerful statements that can transform your mindset and enhance your well-being. Here's a straightforward method to help you structure positive affirmations:

Start with the present tense: Begin your affirmation with words that indicate the present moment, such as "I am" or "I have." This helps to anchor your affirmation in the current reality.

Use positive language: State your affirmation in a positive and empowering manner. Focus on what you want to affirm or attract into your life rather than what you want to avoid or eliminate. This helps shift your mindset towards positivity and possibilities.

Be specific and clear: Make your affirmation specific and clear to give it focus and direction. Instead of vague statements, be precise about the qualities, experiences, or changes you want to affirm.

Use solid and assertive words: Choose powerful words that evoke confidence and conviction. This reinforces the power and impact of your affirmation. Examples of concrete terms include "strong," "capable," "worthy," "deserving," and "abundant."

Make it personal: Tailor your affirmation to your own needs and desires. Use "I" statements to personalize the affirmation and make it more meaningful to you. This reinforces a sense of ownership and self-empowerment.

Emphasize the positive outcome: Focus on the development or result you want to manifest. Visualize and feel the emotions associated with the desired effect as you craft your affirmation. This helps to strengthen your belief and align your energy with the claim.

Repeat and reinforce: Repetition is critical to the effectiveness of affirmations. Repeat your affirmations regularly, ideally daily, to support the positive messages in your subconscious mind. Consistency and repetition help to rewire your thinking patterns and reinforce positive beliefs.

Remember, the power of positive affirmations lies in your belief and intention. Choose affirmations that resonate with you and feel authentic. Experiment with different affirmations and adjust them to reflect your evolving goals and desires. With consistent practice and a positive mindset, affirmations can become a powerful tool for transforming your self-image and enhancing your self-worth.

My Positive Affirmations

My Positive Affirmations

Week 3

Cultivating
Self-Compassion and Gratitude

Self-compassion is extending kindness, understanding, and empathy to oneself, particularly during challenging times, failure, or self-judgment. It involves treating oneself with the same compassion and care that one would offer to a loved one in a similar situation. Here's why self-compassion is essential in your journey.

Self-Acceptance: Self-compassion allows you to accept yourself fully, flaws and all. It recognizes that everyone makes mistakes and experiences challenges, fostering a non-judgmental and nurturing attitude toward yourself. By embracing self-acceptance, you can cultivate a positive self-image and build a stronger foundation of self-worth.

Emotional Resilience: Practicing self-compassion enhances your emotional resilience. It helps you navigate difficult emotions, setbacks, and failures with kindness and understanding. Instead of berating yourself or getting caught in negative self-talk, self-compassion encourages you to acknowledge your pain, offer comfort, and find healthy ways to cope and move forward.

Motivation and Growth: Contrary to popular belief, self-compassion doesn't breed complacency. It fosters motivation and growth. By treating yourself with kindness and encouragement, you create a safe and supportive environment for personal development. Self-compassion enables you to learn from your mistakes, make healthier choices, and take on new challenges without fear of self-criticism or judgment.

Relationships: Self-compassion positively impacts your relationships with others. When you are compassionate toward yourself, you become better equipped to extend that compassion to others. It enhances your ability to empathize, connect, and support others, fostering healthier and more fulfilling relationships.

Gratitude is the practice of acknowledging and appreciating the positive aspects of your life. It involves intentionally focusing on the blessings, experiences, and relationships that bring you joy and fulfilment. Here's why cultivating gratitude is vital in your journey:

Perspective Shift: Gratitude helps shift your perspective from a scarcity mindset to one of abundance. By consciously acknowledging and expressing gratitude for what you have, you train your mind to focus on the positives rather than dwell on the negatives. This shift in perspective can improve your overall well-being and increase your sense of self-worth.

Positive Mindset: Cultivating gratitude nurtures a positive mindset. Regularly reflecting on what you're grateful for invites more positive experiences and emotions into your life. Gratitude enhances your overall mood, reduces stress, and boosts happiness and contentment.

Self-Appreciation: Gratitude allows you to appreciate yourself and your accomplishments. By acknowledging and expressing gratitude for your strengths, achievements, and progress, you reinforce a positive self-image and strengthen your self-worth.

Connection and Empathy: Gratitude fosters a deeper connection with others and promotes empathy. When you express gratitude for the people in your life, you strengthen your relationships and create a sense of community. Gratitude also helps you recognize the contributions and support you receive, encouraging you to reciprocate and extend kindness to others.

I encourage you to embrace self-compassion and gratitude throughout this challenge and practice self-compassion by offering yourself kindness, understanding, and forgiveness during challenging times. Cultivate gratitude by regularly reflecting on and expressing appreciation for the positive aspects of your life. These practices will deepen your self-worth, enhance your well-being, and create a more fulfilling and joyful life journey.

DAYS 13-15 Self-Compassion Exercises

Engage in self-compassion practices such as writing a compassionate letter to yourself, practising self-forgiveness, and treating yourself with kindness and understanding.

Day 13: Loving-Kindness Meditation

Instructions:

You can find a quiet and comfortable space where you can practice undisturbed.

Sit in a relaxed position with your eyes closed or softly focused.

Take a few deep breaths to centre yourself and bring your attention to the present moment.

Begin by directing loving-kindness towards yourself. Repeat the following phrases silently or aloud:

May I be safe and protected.
May I be happy and healthy.
May I be at peace with my body.
May I accept and love myself unconditionally.

As you repeat these phrases, visualize yourself surrounded by a warm, loving light.

Expand the loving-kindness to others, starting with someone you love, then to someone neutral, and finally to someone with whom you have difficulties.

End the meditation by returning your focus to yourself and repeating the self-compassion phrases.

Take a few moments to sit in stillness and feel the loving-kindness radiating within you.

Day 14: Self-Compassion Letter

Instructions:

Set aside dedicated time and find a peaceful space for reflection and writing.

You can begin by acknowledging your negative self-talk or judgments about your body's self-image.

Write a heartfelt letter to yourself, expressing compassion, understanding, and acceptance towards your body and self-image.

Validate any pain, insecurities, or challenges you have faced, and offer yourself words of comfort and reassurance.

Recognize that you are not the only one who has struggled with body self-image, and extend kindness to yourself, knowing you deserve love and acceptance.

Emphasize the qualities, strengths, and achievements unrelated to your physical appearance, acknowledging your worth beyond your body.

Could you finish the letter by expressing forgiveness and a commitment to treat yourself with compassion and kindness going forward?

Please keep the letter safe and reread it whenever you need a reminder of your self-compassion journey.

Day 15: Self-Compassionate Affirmations

Instructions:

Find a quiet space to sit comfortably and focus on your affirmations.

Take a few deep breaths, centre yourself and bring your attention to the present moment.

Could you create a list of self-compassionate affirmations tailored to body self-image and self-worth?

Repeat the affirmations silently or aloud, allowing their empowering and compassionate messages to resonate within you.

As you repeat each affirmation, visualize yourself embodying the qualities and experiences they represent.

Please address any resistance or negative thoughts and counter them with self-compassion and understanding.

Feel the warmth and kindness radiating from within as you embrace these affirmations as valid and deserving of your self-worth.

Please carry the affirmations throughout the day, and recite them whenever you need a reminder of your inherent self-compassion.

Remember, self-compassion is a journey, and it takes time and practice. Be patient and gentle with yourself as you explore these exercises. Feel free to modify the activities to suit your preferences and needs. The goal is to cultivate self-compassion, promote a positive body self-image, and enhance your self-worth through loving-kindness towards yourself.

Journal

DAYS 16-18   Gratitude Practice

Write down three things you are grateful for about your self-image and self-worth daily. Focus on the positive aspects and strengths you possess.

Day 16: Gratitude for Body Functions

Instructions:

Find a quiet and comfortable space where you can reflect without distractions.

Take a few deep breaths to centre yourself and bring your attention to the present moment.

Reflect on the various functions of your body that you are grateful for. It could be your ability to breathe, see, hear, move, or other bodily functions.

Please list at least three body functions you are grateful for and write them down in your journal.

For each body function, please take a moment to deeply appreciate and acknowledge how it contributes to your daily life and well-being.

As you write, you can focus on the sensations and experiences associated with each function, cultivating gratitude and appreciation.

Whenever you encounter challenges or negative thoughts about your body, remind yourself of gratitude for these functions, using them as a source of strength and appreciation.

Journal

Day 17: Gratitude for Body Strength and Resilience

Instructions:

Could you set aside some quiet time for reflection and gratitude practice?

Sit comfortably and close your eyes, allowing yourself to relax and become present.

Consider how your body has shown strength and resilience throughout your life.

Reflect on moments when your body has overcome challenges, healed from injuries, or carried you through difficult times.

Write down at least three instances where you felt your body's strength and resilience and express gratitude for each experience. Focus on the feelings of empowerment, gratitude, and appreciation that arise as you acknowledge your body's capabilities.

Whenever you feel doubt or self-criticism regarding your body, remind yourself of the strength and resilience it has demonstrated, reinforcing a positive body self-image.

You will find a **Gratitude Guide for Body Strength and Resilience** on the following page.

Strong Muscles: Express gratitude for the strength of your muscles that allow you to move, lift, and engage in various physical activities.

Healthy Joints: Be thankful for your joints that enable smooth and pain-free movements, allowing you to walk, run, and perform daily tasks.

Balanced Posture: Appreciate your body's ability to maintain a balanced posture, providing stability and support throughout your daily activities.

Resilient Bones: Acknowledge the resilience of your bones, which provide structure and protect your vital organs, allowing you to lead an active lifestyle.

Energetic Cardiovascular System: Express gratitude for your heart and cardiovascular system, which pumps blood efficiently, supplying oxygen and nutrients to every part of your body.

Flexibility: Be thankful for the flexibility of your body, allowing you to stretch, bend, and move with ease, preventing stiffness and promoting overall well-being.

Sensory Organs: Appreciate your eyes, ears, nose, tongue, and skin, which allow you to experience the world through sight, sound, smell, taste, and touch.

Endurance: Give thanks for your body's endurance, allowing you to persevere through challenges, whether during exercise or facing the demands of daily life.

Recovery Abilities: Acknowledge the body's capacity for recovery and healing, whether from illness, injury, or stress, allowing you to bounce back and continue moving forward.

Adaptive Immune System: Express gratitude for your immune system, which works tirelessly to protect you from infections and illnesses, contributing to your overall health and well-being.

Day 18: Gratitude for Self-Worth and Inner Qualities

Instructions:

Find a peaceful and comfortable space for your gratitude practice.

Take a few deep breaths to centre yourself and bring awareness to the present moment.

I'd like you to reflect on the qualities, traits, and inner strengths that you appreciate about yourself beyond physical appearance.

Write down at least three qualities or aspects of your personality that you are grateful for, focusing on your self-worth and inner beauty.

As you write, allow yourself to truly feel the gratitude and appreciation for these qualities, acknowledging their significance in shaping who you are.

Recognize that your self-worth extends far beyond your body and physical appearance, and celebrate the unique qualities that make you who you are.

Whenever you encounter self-doubt or negative thoughts about your body self-image, remind yourself of gratitude for your self-worth and inner qualities, nurturing a positive and empowering sense of self.

Remember, gratitude is a practice that can be cultivated over time. Be patient and kind to yourself as you explore these gratitude exercises. Feel free to adapt the prompts and tips to suit your preferences and needs. The goal is to foster a deeper appreciation for your body, enhance your self-worth, and cultivate a positive body self-image through the power of gratitude.

Week 4

Empowering Actions and Environment

Actions are crucial in shaping our beliefs, thoughts, and self-perception.

Here's how they contribute to the process:

Behavioural Reinforcement: Our actions can reinforce or challenge our beliefs and thoughts. When we consistently engage in behaviours that align with opposing beliefs, we strengthen those beliefs and perpetuate a cycle of negativity. However, by consciously choosing actions that reflect self-compassion, gratitude, and self-worth, we can challenge and reshape our beliefs, fostering personal growth and positive change.

Self-Discovery: Taking intentional actions allows us to explore our strengths, interests, and values. By engaging in activities that align with our authentic selves, we gain a deeper understanding of who we are and what brings us joy and fulfilment. These self-discovery actions help us develop a stronger sense of self-worth and self-identity.

Breaking Patterns: Actions allow breaking free from self-sabotaging patterns and behaviours. By consciously choosing actions that align with our desired self-image and self-worth, we can interrupt negative cycles and create new, healthier habits. Each positive step reinforces our belief in our ability to make positive changes and contributes to our personal growth.

Role Models: Our environment often presents us with role models who embody the qualities, beliefs, and behaviours we aspire to have. By observing and learning from these individuals, we can gain inspiration and guidance on cultivating self-compassion, gratitude, and self-worth in our own lives. However, it's essential to recognize that those who do not embody the qualities we want to have can also offer valuable insights.

When we encounter individuals who don't align with the qualities we desire, we can view it as an opportunity to observe what we do not want in our lives. It's an opportunity for self-reflection, allowing us to gain clarity on our values, boundaries, and the kind of person we strive to be. Without judgment or criticism, we can acknowledge that everyone is on their own personal growth journey, and their actions reflect their challenges and experiences.

By observing what doesn't resonate with us, we gain a deeper understanding of our authentic desires and the direction we want to take in our personal growth. It reinforces our commitment to cultivating self-compassion, gratitude, and self-worth as we consciously embody the qualities that align with our values and aspirations.

On this journey of personal growth, positive role models and those who challenge our ideals serve as valuable teachers. They provide contrasting experiences highlighting the path we want to follow and the attributes we want to cultivate within ourselves. By remaining open and receptive, we can learn from both sides of the spectrum, refining our beliefs and behaviours.

Remember, this is a journey of self-discovery, and the observations we make about others serve as a mirror for our growth. Embrace the opportunity to observe, reflect, and reaffirm your desires and aspirations. With compassion and understanding, allow these encounters to guide you in pursuing self-compassion, gratitude, and self-worth, knowing that each experience contributes to your personal growth and transformation.

So, alongside the positive role models, recognize the valuable lessons offered by those who don't align with your ideals. Embrace these moments of contrast as opportunities for self-reflection and reaffirmation, and continue to shape your path with authenticity and grace.

Environmental Triggers: Our environment can trigger or reinforce negative beliefs and thoughts. For example, an environment that constantly supports beauty standards or promotes comparison can intensify negative self-perceptions. Recognizing and actively managing these environmental triggers is essential in our journey of personal growth. Creating an environment that supports self-compassion and gratitude can help counteract negative influences. Our environment significantly influences our beliefs, thoughts, and self-perception. Here's how it contributes to the process:

Surrounding ourselves with a supportive and nurturing environment can facilitate personal growth and transformation. When people believe in us, encourage our self-compassion and gratitude practices, and provide a safe space for self-expression, it becomes easier to challenge negative beliefs and foster positive change. However, even without a supportive environment, we can harness our inner strength and use it as an opportunity for growth.

In the face of a not-so-supportive environment, we can view it as a challenge that tests our resilience and inner fortitude. It becomes an opportunity to shift deeper into our emotional healing journey and question why unsupportive attitudes or actions trigger us. By exploring our triggers, we gain insight into our wounds, fears, and insecurities that may still require healing and self-compassion.

Challenging environments can be transformative catalysts for self-reflection and growth. They push us to cultivate inner strength, self-belief, and self-validation. As we navigate these challenging spaces, we learn to rely on our internal resources, assert our boundaries, and develop a deeper understanding of our worthiness.

By recognizing that triggers from an unsupportive environment indicate areas of emotional healing and self-exploration, we empower ourselves to take charge of our growth.

Ultimately, personal growth is about embracing our strength, resilience, and the capacity to create positive change within ourselves, regardless of external circumstances. Through these challenges, we grow, heal, and forge a path of self-discovery and empowerment.

So, in addition to cultivating a supportive environment, let us acknowledge the power we hold within ourselves to navigate and overcome the trials of an unsupportive environment. Embrace this opportunity for self-reflection, inner strength, and healing, as it strengthens your resilience and propels you forward on your growth journey.

Personal Space: Our physical space can also impact our mindset and well-being. Creating a unique space that reflects our values, inspires positivity, and fosters self-care can enhance our self-compassion and gratitude practices. It becomes a sanctuary to engage in reflection, self-care activities, and mindfulness, supporting our personal growth.

By consciously aligning our actions with our desired beliefs and creating an environment that supports our personal growth, we create a robust foundation for transformation. Through intentional actions and a supportive environment for self-compassion and gratitude, we reinforce positive beliefs, challenge negative thoughts, and nurture our self-worth.

I encourage you to take intentional actions that align with your desired self-image and self-worth. Surround yourself with a supportive environment and create a personal space that nurtures growth. By considering the role of actions and environment, you enhance your ability to cultivate self-compassion, gratitude, and a positive self-perception on your transformation journey.

Days 19-21 Actionable Goals

Set three specific and achievable goals that contribute to your self-image and self-worth. Break them down into smaller steps and work on them throughout the week.

Some examples you can integrate into your day:

Engage in daily affirmations: Set a goal to incorporate positive affirmations into your daily routine. Choose empowering statements that uplift your self-image and reinforce your self-worth. For example, "I will say three affirmations every morning to remind myself of my worthiness and inner strength."

Practice self-care rituals: Make it a goal to prioritize self-care activities that nourish your mind, body, and soul. This can include taking regular walks in nature, practising mindfulness or meditation, indulging in a hobby you love, or dedicating time for self-reflection and journaling. For instance, "I will dedicate at least 30 minutes each day to engage in self-care practices that enhance my self-image and reinforce my self-worth."

Seek support and personal development resources: Set a goal to actively seek resources to support your personal growth and help improve your self-image and self-worth. This can include books, podcasts, online courses, or therapy/coaching sessions if you feel guided to this. For example, "I will commit to reading one self-help book monthly to deepen my self-understanding and enhance my self-worth."

Actionable goals should be specific, measurable, achievable, relevant, and time-bound (SMART). Tailor these examples to fit your circumstances and ensure they align with your values and aspirations.

Days 22-24 Environment Cleanse

Declutter your physical space, eliminating items that no longer serve you. Create an environment that reflects your positive self-image and promotes self-worth.

Start with small areas: Begin your decluttering journey by tackling small areas or specific categories, such as a drawer, a shelf, or a particular type of item. This helps build momentum and prevents overwhelm.

Use the "One In, One Out" rule: For every new item you bring into your space, commit to removing one thing. This helps maintain a balanced and clutter-free environment, preventing unnecessary accumulation.

Declutter regularly: Set aside dedicated time each month or season to declutter and reorganize your living spaces. Regular decluttering sessions prevent clutter from accumulating and make maintaining a clean and organized environment easier.

Create designated spaces: Assign specific areas for different items, such as a designated spot for keys, a bin for mail, or shelves for books. Having designated spaces helps prevent things from getting scattered and makes it easier to find what you need.

Let go of sentimental attachments: While it can be challenging, letting go of items with sentimental value that no longer serve a purpose in your life can create more space and clarity. You can consider taking photos of sentimental items before parting with them to ensure the memories are safe.

Day 22: Decluttering Physical Space

Instructions:

Choose a specific area in your living space directly linked to your body's self-image and self-worth, such as your bedroom, bathroom or kitchen.

Take 15 minutes to declutter and organize this space. Remove any items that trigger negative thoughts or emotions about your body and self-worth.

Create a clean and inviting environment by tidying up, arranging items to promote a positive body image, and adding elements that make you feel good about yourself, such as inspirational quotes or affirmations.

Dispose of, sell, or donate any clothing that no longer fits or makes you uncomfortable, and consider removing unhealthy foods and snacks from your pantry to support a healthier lifestyle.

As you clean and declutter, reflect on how this physical transformation positively impacts your mindset and self-perception.

Day 23: Digital Cleanse

Instructions:

You can use the time to declutter your digital environment, focusing on areas that influence your body's self-image and self-worth, such as social media or online content.

Unfollow or mute social media accounts that promote opposing body ideals or trigger comparison and self-doubt.

Seek and follow accounts promoting body positivity, self-acceptance, and self-love.

Review your digital photo albums and reflect on pictures that make you feel insecure or remind you of negative body experiences. Try to be as non-judgemental as possible and use self-compassion and acceptance to shift your emotional perception of your body's self-image. You can also opt to delete any photos you wish to part with.

Customize your online experience by adjusting privacy settings and limiting exposure to harmful or triggering content.

Notice how these changes in your digital environment contribute to a more positive and supportive mindset regarding your body.

Day 24: Social Circle Evaluation

Instructions:

Reflect on the people in your social circle and their impact on your body, self-image and self-worth.

Identify individuals who consistently uplift and support you, and make an effort to deepen those connections.

Set boundaries with individuals who perpetuate negative body talk or engage in body shaming behaviours.

Consider seeking body-positive communities or support groups that align with your values and provide a safe space for self-expression.

Engage in conversations with your trusted friends or loved ones about body positivity and self-acceptance, fostering a supportive and empowering environment.

Notice the influence of your social circle on your self-perception and take steps to surround yourself with people who celebrate and appreciate you for who you are.

Remember, an environment cleanse creates a space that nurtures a positive body self-image and self-worth. Customize these tips to suit your needs and preferences. Be mindful of the impact that your physical space, digital environment, and social circle have on your mindset and make intentional choices that support your well-being and self-growth.

Week 5

Integration and Celebration

Integration involves the process of unifying and harmonizing various aspects of ourselves, our experiences, and our growth. It encompasses the following:

Embracing Wholeness: Integration invites us to embrace the full spectrum of our being, the light and the shadow, the strengths and the areas for growth. It's about acknowledging that all parts of ourselves have a purpose and deserve acceptance. We cultivate a sense of inner harmony and authenticity by integrating these aspects.

Learning from Experiences: Integration allows us to learn from positive and challenging experiences. It involves reflecting on our past, extracting wisdom, and integrating those lessons into our present and future actions. We transform our experiences into valuable stepping stones for personal growth by combining them.

Aligning Mind, Heart, and Body: Integration involves aligning our thoughts, emotions, and physical actions. It's about listening to the wisdom of our hearts, honouring the intelligence of our bodies, and engaging our minds in a balanced and harmonious way. By integrating these aspects, we encourage greater self-awareness and alignment.

Embracing Change: Integration embraces change as an inherent part of personal growth. It allows us to navigate life's transitions and challenges with grace and adaptability. Rather than resisting change, integration enables us to embrace it, learn from it, and integrate the lessons into our evolving selves.

Celebration joyously acknowledges and honours our progress, achievements, and milestones. Here's why celebration is vital:

Gratitude and Appreciation: Celebration expresses gratitude and appreciation for ourselves and our journey. It allows us to recognize the efforts we've put forth, the growth we've experienced, and the positive changes we've made. Celebration cultivates a mindset of gratitude, amplifying our joy and sense of fulfilment.

Positive Reinforcement: Celebrating our wins reinforces positive behaviours and beliefs. It acknowledges and validates our efforts, motivating us to continue on the path of personal growth. Celebration strengthens our self-belief, enhances our self-worth, and encourages us to reach even greater heights.

Reflection and Integration: Celebration provides an opportunity for reflection and integration. It allows us to pause, reflect on our progress, and integrate the lessons and growth into our self-perception. We acknowledge our journey's significance by celebrating, reinforcing positive changes and fostering a sense of wholeness.

Joy and Well-being: Celebration is a pathway to pleasure and well-being. It infuses our lives with positivity, uplifts our spirits, and nourishes our souls. By actively engaging in celebrations, we enhance our overall well-being, foster self-compassion, and nurture a deep sense of self-love and appreciation.

Incorporating integration and celebration into your growth journey empowers you to live a more vibrant and fulfilling life. Embrace the integration process, honouring all aspects of yourself and learning from your experiences. Then, celebrate your progress, achievements, and the person you're becoming. Integrating and celebrating create a joyful and harmonious path to self-discovery, growth, and fulfilment.

I encourage you to actively integrate your experiences, align your mind, heart, and body, and celebrate your victories along the way. Embrace the journey with gratitude, joy, and celebration, knowing you continually evolve into your most authentic and empowered self.

Days 25-27: Positive Reinforcement

Review your progress and celebrate the positive changes you've experienced. Acknowledge and reinforce your new empowering beliefs and thoughts.

Some simple ideas for celebrating your progress:

Treat yourself to a small indulgence: Acknowledge your progress and treat yourself to something that brings you joy. It could be as simple as enjoying a favourite dessert, buying a new book or movie you've been wanting, or taking a relaxing bath with your favourite scented candles.

Gather with loved ones: Celebrate your progress by sharing it with those who support and uplift you. Arrange a small gathering or a virtual hangout with friends or family to share your achievements. Enjoy good company, laughter, and positive energy.

Engage in a self-care activity: Dedicate some time to yourself and engage in a self-care activity that rejuvenates and nourishes your mind, body, and soul. It could be going for a nature walk, practising yoga or meditation, enjoying a spa day at home, or taking a leisurely day off to engage in activities that bring you peace and happiness.

Remember, the celebration is about acknowledging and honouring your progress, big or small. It's an opportunity to express gratitude for your efforts and to recharge for the next steps on your journey of growth and self-improvement.

Days 28-30: Reflection and Future Planning

Reflect on the insights gained during the challenge. Identify ongoing practices to sustain your progress and outline future steps for personal growth.

Identify areas for growth: Reflect on areas where you feel there is room for development and improvement in your self-worth and self-image. Be honest about limiting beliefs or self-sabotaging patterns that may hold you back. This awareness sets the stage for future planning and goal setting.

Set empowering goals: Based on your reflections, set empowering and actionable plans that align with your self-worth and self-image. Make them specific, measurable, attainable, relevant, and time-bound (SMART). These goals should challenge you to step outside your comfort zone and foster personal growth.

Vision Board: Create a visual representation of your desired body image and self-worth by making a vision board. Gather pictures, quotes, and affirmations that inspire and uplift you. Place them on a poster board or a digital collage to serve as a visual reminder of your goals and aspirations.

Visualize your future self: Take time to visualize your ideal future self, someone who embodies a strong sense of self-worth and a positive self-image. Envision the qualities, beliefs, and actions of this empowered version of yourself. Use this vision as inspiration and motivation to guide your future planning and decision-making.

Remember, reflection and future planning are ongoing processes. Continuously assess your progress, adjust your goals, and maintain a growth mindset. Embrace the power of self-reflection to fuel your self-worth, self-image, and overall self-empowerment journey.

Read after you have completed your 30-day challenge!

Congratulations on completing the empowering 30-day challenge with Healthy Patterns Club!

You've embarked on a transformative journey of self-discovery, growth, and personal empowerment. As we wrap up this chapter, let's reflect on your incredible progress and celebrate your achievements.

Throughout these 30 days, you have shown remarkable dedication, courage, and resilience. You've embraced self-compassion and gratitude and challenged negative beliefs with unwavering determination. You've cultivated awareness and reflection and integrated powerful practices into your daily life. Your commitment to your personal growth and well-being is truly inspiring.

You've explored the depths of your inner world, uncovering hidden strengths, unravelling limiting beliefs, and embracing your authentic self. You've discovered the power of self-compassion, nurturing a kinder and gentler relationship with yourself. You've harnessed the magic of gratitude, illuminating the beauty and abundance in your life. You've challenged negative beliefs, rewritten the script of your self-perception, and empowered yourself with a positive mindset.

I want to acknowledge your progress, applaud your efforts, and celebrate the incredible person you are and are still becoming.

Remember, this journey doesn't end here. You have developed powerful tools and practices to continue supporting your growth and personal evolution. As you move forward, carry the lessons and insights you've gained, knowing you can create a life that aligns with your most authentic desires and highest aspirations.

Celebrate this milestone and bask in the joy of your accomplishments. Take a moment to acknowledge the progress you've made, the challenges you've overcome, and the person you've become. Embrace your worthiness, your authenticity, and your inherent potential.

As you step into the next phase of your journey, remember to be kind to yourself, celebrate your wins (both big and small), and continue to nurture self-compassion and gratitude. Know that you have the power to create a life filled with purpose, joy, and fulfilment.

Congratulations once again on completing this transformative 30-day challenge. You are an inspiration, and I am honoured to be part of your journey. Embrace the possibilities that lie ahead, and continue to shine your light brightly as you navigate the beautiful path of personal growth and self-discovery.

Here's to your ongoing success, happiness, and an empowered life beyond your wildest dreams.

You've got this!

Terms of use

This challenge is designed for personal growth and self-empowerment purposes.
It is not intended to replace professional therapy or medical advice.
While the exercises and practices included in this challenge can benefit personal development, they should not substitute for professional guidance when dealing with mental health concerns or other significant issues.
Participants engaging in this challenge do so voluntarily and assume full responsibility for their own well-being and personal growth journey. Healthy Patterns Club, Apolonia Wieland and any associated entities or individuals involved in the creation of this challenge are not liable for any damages, losses, or consequences arising from the use of the materials or implementation of the practices provided.
By participating in this challenge, you acknowledge and agree to respect the materials' copyright, use them solely for personal reasons, and understand that they are not a substitute for professional therapy or medical advice.
If you have any questions or concerns about the challenge materials' usage, distribution, or reproduction, please don't hesitate to contact selfhelpdesk@healthypatterns.club for further clarification.
Thank you for your understanding and adherence to these guidelines.

Apolonia, **HealthyPatterns.Club**

Copyright Notice:

Mindfulness is Self-Empowerment!

#healthypatternsclubforkids

SCAN ME

Empower your child with the transformative potential of mindfulness! Practising mindfulness can help kids develop emotional regulation, increase attention and focus, reduce stress and anxiety, and improve overall well-being. Mindfulness teaches children to live in the present moment, cultivate self-awareness, and build resilience. Our tailored prompts for gratitude, positive self-talk, and self-care provide the perfect starting point for mindfulness practice. By encouraging your child to practice mindfulness regularly, you can help them build lifelong habits for a happy and healthy life. Give your child the gift of mindfulness and help them unlock their full potential!

Now Available in Paperback!

Printed in Great Britain
by Amazon

36716460R00079